LADY LIBERTY ENLIGHTENS THE WORLD

INTERESTING FACTS ABOUT THE STATUE OF LIBERTY

American History for Kids
Children's History Books

BABY PROFESSOR
EDUCATION KIDS

Speedy Publishing LLC

40 E. Main St. #1156

Newark, DE 19711

www.speedypublishing.com

Copyright 2017

In this book, we're going to cover interesting facts about the Statue of Liberty. So, let's get right to it!

WHAT IS THE STATUE OF LIBERTY?

The Statue of Liberty is a giant statue of a woman with a crown on her head and a torch in her hands. She stands majestically at the entrance to New York Harbor on a small island now called Liberty Island.

Her design, especially her free-flowing robe, was influenced by the Ancient Roman goddess called Libertas who represented liberty from tyranny and was worshipped in Rome as the goddess of freed slaves.

IT STARTED WITH A DINNER IN FRANCE

The year is 1865 and a stately dinner is being held in France. At that dinner a group of men are discussing the dictatorship in France. They admire the American government and the freedom of its democracy.

They discuss how they would like to give a 100th birthday present to the United States. The two governments have been friends for a long time. This gift will make a statement about how democracy should also be the government in France.

A young French sculptor by the name of Frédéric-Auguste Bartholdi overhears them. He gets very excited about designing this statue. He starts to sketch drawings of a giant statue holding a torch of freedom. He models the face of the statue after his mother and hopes that it can be built out of copper.

From Bartholdi's initial idea, it took 21 years before the statue was designed, financed, and built, but he did not give up. He was the first to be inspired by the vision of the Lady of Liberty, but this was just the beginning of her influence.

BARTHOLDI TRAVELS TO AMERICA

Bartholdi traveled to America to get financing for the Statue of Liberty. He traveled by ship and when he got to New York Harbor he noticed a small island that was the perfect spot for the statue.

At that time, huge numbers of people were coming to America from other countries because they wanted to be free. The Statue of Liberty would be the first thing they saw when they entered their new country.

Bartholdi spent five months traveling the country and started the Franco-American union to raise money for the statue. He needed to raise $400,000. In today's currency, that would be over $7 million dollars.

BARTHOLDI HIRES EIFFEL

Bartholdi had the vision for how the Statue of Liberty should look, but he still needed someone to build the huge statue. Someone who understood the engineering of how such a massive structure could be built. He chose Gustave Eiffel, the engineer who would later design the famous Eiffel tower in Paris.

Bartholdi and Eiffel set to work but as they went along they kept running out of money and had to stop working until they could raise more. In America the same thing was happening. Congress decided that they wouldn't help pay for the statue's stand. That's when a famous newspaper editor by the name of Joseph Pulitzer stepped in.

JOSEPH PULITZER

He wrote about the statue in his paper so that people would help. Over 120,000 people across the US donated. They each gave about 83 cents. Children helped raise money too. Pulitzer publicized that children had given up money that they had saved to go to the circus.

HOW AND WHEN WAS THE STATUE CONSTRUCTED?

The engineering required to build the statue in France and have it transported to the United States was staggering. Eiffel came up with the idea of giving the statue an iron spine and framework made of metal.

GUSTAVE EIFFEL

The thin copper skin, less than 1/8 of an inch thick, about the thickness of two pennies, is attached to this framework. The green color is due to the oxidation of the natural copper color. Although this coating called a patina is a sign of damage to the copper, it also protects the statue from further erosion.

The project was officially announced in 1875. The arm with the torch attached was constructed first and was presented to the audience at the Centennial Exhibition, which took place in 1876 in Philadelphia. Next, the head was finished and was displayed at the World's Fair in Paris in 1878. The remaining portions of the statue were built over the next several years. Everything was made in sections.

Sections were ready to be shipped from France to the United States in 1885 and the statue almost didn't make it there when the ship transporting it got into stormy seas. In the spring of 1886, the assembly started.

The iron frame that Eiffel had proposed was constructed and the copper pieces were hammered in over the top of that frame. The official dedication took place on October 28, 1886.

WHAT DOES SHE STAND FOR?

There are many symbols in the design of the Statue of Liberty. Her official name is "Liberty Enlightening the World." Her torch carries the light that illuminates and inspires people around the world for the desire to be free. She came to be an icon for what America stands for, a free country ruled by and for the people.

At her feet are broken chains to represent the freedom from oppression of all types. She steps confidently out of those chains, knowing that she will never allow herself to be imprisoned by tyranny again.

She holds a tablet in her left hand. It symbolizes that the United States is built on laws. In fact, the shape of the tablet is a keystone. In architecture, a keystone is a stone that keeps the other stones together. This symbol represents that the laws governing the United States are what keep our country strong and are the foundation upon which our country is built.

Originally the tablet was left blank, but Bartholdi added the date of America's independence from Great Britain, July 4, 1776. The date is written in Roman numerals to once again highlight the laws upon which the country is built. The twenty-five windows in her crown represent the rays of heavenly light that shine down upon America.

Some people believe that the seven rays in the statue's crown stand for the seven continents and seven seas. Others believe that these rays represent rays from the sun and suggest a divine halo.

The stand also has some symbolism attached to it. It's made from thirteen different types of granite, one type for every colony in early America. The stand has shields on each side, which symbolize the states in the Union.

WHAT IS THE HEIGHT AND WEIGHT OF THE STATUE OF LIBERTY?

The height of the entire statue from the base of the statue to the very tip of her torch is 305.5 feet. Her height from the bottom of her feet to the top of her head is 111.5 feet. Her weight is 450,000 pounds, which is equivalent to 225 tons. Her face measures 8 feet tall.

FASCINATING FACTS ABOUT THE STATUE OF LIBERTY

- ➲ The French people paid for the Statue itself and the American people paid for the statue's stand.

- ➲ In 1984, Lady Liberty's torch was replaced by a new torch made of copper and completely covered in 24-carat gold leaf.

⮕ The Statue of Liberty became known as the "Mother of Exiles." Over 9 million immigrants came to the United States during the last half of the 19th century.

⮕ The colossal statue was a memorable beginning to those who wanted to make America their home.

➲ When there are winds of 50 miles per hour or more, she sways up to three inches and her torch moves as much as five inches.

➲ When the statue was first put up in 1886, it had the distinction of being the tallest structure made of iron ever built.

- Two images of the Statue of Liberty are printed on the $10 bill.
- In 1984, UNESCO announced that the Statue of Liberty had made its list of World Heritage Sites.
- There's a replica of the statue on the Las Vegas Strip and one in Paris as well.

- If a shoemaker were hired to make shoes for her, they would have to be a size 879.
- If she wore a belt, it would need to be about 35 feet in length.
- In order to create the copper part of the structure, three hundred various types of hammers were needed.

VISITING THE STATUE OF LIBERTY TODAY

About 4 million tourists visit the statue every year and go up the 354 steps to get to the crown. One of the most popular tourist sites in the US, the Statue of Liberty continues to inspire people all over the world with the desire to secure freedom.

Awesome! Now you know more about how Lady Liberty represents freedom to people around the world. You can find more American History books from Baby Professor by searching the website of your favorite book retailer.

Visit

BABY PROFESSOR
EDUCATION KIDS

www.BabyProfessorBooks.com

to download Free Baby Professor eBooks
and view our catalog of new and exciting
Children's Books

Made in the USA
Monee, IL
21 December 2021